# THE SCRAPBOOKER'S CREATIVITY KIT!

## Prompts and ideas to jump start your layouts

Claudine **Hellmuth**

**MEMORY MAKERS BOOKS**

Cincinnati, Ohio
www.mycraftivity.com

# About the Author

Claudine Hellmuth is a nationally recognized collage artist, author and illustrator. She combines photos, paint, paper and pen into quirky, whimsical, retro collages she calls Poppets®. Her artwork has been featured on *The Martha Stewart Show*, in Mary Engelbreit's *Home Companion* magazine, on HGTV's *I Want That!* and on the DIY Network's *Craft Lab*. In addition to creating her artwork full-time, Claudine teaches collage workshops in the U.S. and Canada, and she has written two other books, *Collage Discovery Workshop* and *Collage Discovery Workshop: Beyond the Unexpected* (North Light Books). She has also produced three instructional DVD workshops. Claudine's home studio is in Washington, D.C., where she lives with her husband, Paul, and their very spoiled pets Toby the wonder dog and Mable and Stanley the cats.

Visit her Web site at *www.collageartist.com* and blog at *www.claudinehellmuth.blogspot.com*

**The Scrapbooker's Creativity Kit.** Copyright © 2009 by Claudine Hellmuth. Manufactured in China. All rights reserved. It is permissible for the purchaser to make the projects contained herein and sell them at fairs, bazaars and craft shows. No other part of this book may be reproduced in any form or by any electronic or mechanical means including information storage and retrieval systems without permission in writing from the publisher, except by a reviewer, who may quote a brief passage in review. Published by Memory Makers Books, an imprint of F+W Publications, Inc., 4700 East Galbraith Road, Cincinnati, Ohio 45236. (800) 289-0963. First edition.

13  12  11  10  09    5  4  3  2  1

Distributed in Canada by Fraser Direct
100 Armstrong Avenue
Georgetown, ON, Canada  L7G 5S4
Tel: (905) 877-4411

Distributed in the U.K. and Europe by David & Charles
Brunel House, Newton Abbot, Devon, TQ12 4PU, England
Tel: (+44) 1626 323200, Fax: (+44) 1626 323319
E-mail: postmaster@davidandcharles.co.uk

Distributed in Australia by Capricorn Link
P.O. Box 704, S. Windsor, NSW 2756 Australia
Tel: (02) 4577-3555

Library of Congress Cataloging-in-Publication Data

Hellmuth, Claudine
  Scrapbooker's creativity kit / Claudine Hellmuth. -- 1st ed.
     p. cm.
  ISBN 978-1-59963-031-1 (pbk. : alk. paper)
  1.  Photograph albums. 2.  Scrapbooking. 3.  Photographs--Conservation and restoration.  I. Title.
   TR501.H45 2009
   745.593--dc22

                                        2008023744

Editor: Kristin Boys
Designer: Corrie Schaffeld
Art Coordinator: Eileen Aber
Production Coordinator: Greg Nock
Illustrator: Rob Warnick
Photographer: Tim Grondin

F+W PUBLICATIONS, INC.

www.fwpublications.com

# The Players

## Design Team:
Kal Barteski
Ashley Calder
Donna Downey
Rhonna Farrer
Claudine Hellmuth
Christina Lazar-Schuler
Genevieve Simmonds

## Gallery Contributors:
Michelle Bernard-Harmazinski
www.yesterdaystrashart.com

Sarah Bowen
www.sarahbowen.typepad.com

Kelli Darr
www.darrfamily.typepad.com

Courtney DeLaura
www.peachtree-studio.com

Diane Dolan
www.lifeiwantin.blogspot.com

Jody Ferlaak
www.jodyferlaak.blogspot.com

Wilna Furstenberg
www.wilnaf.com

Lisa Garay
www.lisa-garay.blogspot.com

Bernadette Henderson
www.b3designs.blogspot.com

Jeanette Herdman
www.jeanetteherdman.com

Gigi Kennedy
www.gigikennedy.typepad.com

Adrienne Looman
www.aloomanart.com

Gretchen McElveen
www.gretchenmac.blogspot.com

Melanie McFarlin
www.melaniemcfarlin.blogspot.com

Celine Navarro
www.thegreenfrogstudio.typepad.com

Becky Novacek
www.beckynovacek.typepad.com

Becky Olsen
www.lifeasathreeleggeddog.blogspot.com

Michelle Ramirez
www.flyingmichelle.blogspot.com

Becca Sutton
www.randomthoughtsbybecca.blogspot.com

Jo-Anne te Raa
www.bebebloemetje.typepad.com

Kayla Aimee Terrell
www.kaylaaimee.typepad.com

Andrea Wiebe
www.andreawiebe.com

Ashley Wren
www.sandlian.blogspot.com

Kerry Lynn Yeary
www.k8tykat.typepad.com

# How to Use This Kit

Take your thoughts on a walk. Start with a word. Brainstorm and make lists. See where you are led. You never know where you will end up—and that is half the fun.

I have been using this word prompt technique for jump-starting ideas since 1995. At the beginning of my junior year in college, we did a similar exercise to help us get started after summer break. I have adjusted it a little bit for my own preferences, but ever since then I have been hooked!

This method works every time for generating creative energy. Sometimes I draw a card and I think, "Oh, that's a hard one," or "I really don't like that." But even just knowing that I don't like the prompt can be a starting point for brainstorming something new.

To begin, shuffle the word and color prompt cards separately, then draw one of each. You'll notice that each word prompt card has two words on a side. The idea is to use the word that is facing up when you deal the cards. You might decide to draw two color cards plus one word card as I did for the sample prompts in this book.

Now, let's say you draw *food* + *pink* + *red*. You would need to create a project that had something to do with food (even loosely!) using red and pink somewhere in your piece. You can create whatever interpretation of the three elements your imagination desires! You might choose to do a layout about your favorite food, your child's favorite food or something that you would like to be your child's favorite food (like green beans). If you don't like pink and red

together, you might decide to test the limits of the challenge and squeeze in a teeny tiny bit of pink or small bit of red along with more appealing colors. But you could also decide to use only pink and red. Remember, there are no rules!

As you'll see, the design team came up with lots of interpretations of the six sample prompts featured in this book. Flip through these pages to see how many different directions you can go with a prompt. Then get started on your own projects.

The goal of this kit is to jump-start ideas. Using the kit will give you new ways to think of starting points for your layouts, journaling or other art projects. Don't be frustrated if you can't think of anything right away when you draw the cards. For the *shine* sample prompt, it took me a week to generate an idea that I liked. Give yourself time. The prompts aren't there to rush you but to guide you.

Need more of a challenge? Set a timer for 30 minutes and create something in just that half-hour. Nothing gets the creative juices flowing like the adrenaline rush of working quickly.

Sometimes to get unstuck all we need is a starting point. So get started and see just how far one word can take you!

# Food + Pink + Red

What do sushi, daydreams and a trip to New Zealand have in common? They are all ideas generated by the prompt *food* and the colors pink and red. You'd think a word like *food* would conjure up some pretty obvious ideas. Nope! Take a look at these creations, then take a cue from the designers and let your imagination take you far from where you normally go. I think you'll enjoy all the variations on this yummy theme.

## Claudine Hellmuth

First, I thought of my favorite foods. But then I decided to try another angle. I went with a food that my mom would have wished was my favorite: Brussels sprouts! I wasn't too hot on the idea of pink and red along with the theme so I worked the colors into just some of the details. When I showed the final creation to my mom, she laughed out loud!

**Supplies:** Canvas (Art Alternatives); papers (American Crafts, My Mind's Eye, Provo Craft); acrylic paint, glue, pen (Claudine Hellmuth Studio by Ranger)

### Genevieve Simmonds

I thought of two great tastes that are perfect together: sushi and beer (my favorite pair!).
I took a few photos at a sushi restaurant and then went home to play. I love working
with graph paper and office supplies, so I used a page of graph paper as my background.
A brush of red paint made the perfect base to layer my photos on top.

**Supplies:** Patterned paper (Scenic Route); letter stamps (Fontwerks); sequins (Doodlebug); paint (Making
Memories); Misc: mesh

harpers' woodfired salsa

my favorite restaurant appetizer...
it is the best salsa i have ever had and will
drive 45 minutes just to eat it.

Donna Downey

When I read the prompt, I immediately said, "Let's go get some salsa at Harpers." I brought my camera and took a photo before we ate. Yummy! I came home and took out all the red and pink things in my studio, then I played around to see what would work to create my ode to Harpers' salsa!

**Supplies:** Cardstock (Bazzill); chipboard swirls (Maya Road); floss (DMC); acrylic paint (Chroma); pin (Heidi Grace); DD font (Donna Downey); Misc: dictionary page, felt heart

9

**PRIDE OF SZEGED**

YU mMy

CHICKEN

My favorite authentic food

is Mom's Chicken Paprikash

Mmmm... so

made with REAL Hungarian Paprika

GOOD

**HUNGARIAN**

EXQUISITE 100% SWEET DELICACY

**PAPRIKA**

Christina Lazar-Schuler

My mom always cooked meals from the "homeland" of Hungary, and red reminded me of the rich, orange-red color of Hungary's most famous spice: paprika. As I started working, the red tin container that holds authentic Hungarian paprika popped into my head, so I used the strong red, white and black graphics on the tin as my jumping-off point.

**Supplies:** Papers (Lazar StudioWerx); chipboard letters and tags (Heidi Swapp); Misc: CD tin, office labels, paprika label, pen

Rhonna Farrer

One of the best memories of our New Zealand trip was of the food. We loved the fish 'n' chips shops we came acoss, and I documented one fun adventure with this photo taken in an outdoor shop. The doilies reminded me of food, so I layered them and added the playful transparent image over top.

**Supplies:** Cardstock (Bazzill); rub-ons (Autumn Leaves); stamps (7gypsies, Autumn Leaves); decorative tape (Two's Company); digital accents by Rhonna Farrer (Two Peas in a Bucket); Misc: doilies, pen, transparency

### Ashley Calder

Thinking of food, I cycled through various food-related topics: my grandma's raspberries, growing to-matoes in my garden, weight and body image. Then I remembered the year or two I was vegan. I didn't have any photos at all related to my time as a vegan, so instead I created whimsical illustrations.

**Supplies:** Cardstock (Bazzil); patterned paper (Anna Griffin, Autumn Leaves); letter stickers (Making Memories); chipboard numbers (Heidi Swapp); gold leaf (Stewart Superior); artist's crayons (Caran d'Ache); floss (DMC); watercolor paint and paper (Winsor & Newton); tag (Avery); label holder (Creative Imaginations); decorative scissors (Provo Craft); transparency (Autumn Leaves); rub-ons (BasicGrey); pen and ink (Speedball); Misc: fruit charms, gesso, glass beads

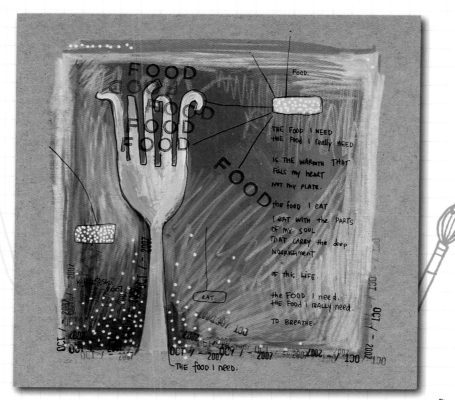

Kal Barteski

I haven't been very hungry lately, so I couldn't think of a food. But I did think of what I've been devouring instead of food. Books. Painting. Writing. Friends. Daydreams. All of the other things that fill me up and bring me peace and inspiration are as important as the breath and energy that I gain from food.

**Supplies:** Chipboard; colored pencils (Prismacolor); acrylic paint (Chroma); ink, stamps (Martha Stewart); pen (Sanford)

# Gallery

 **Jeanette Herdman**

**Supplies:** Overlays (Hambly); letter stickers (American Crafts); decorative tape (Scrap In Style); rhinestones (Heidi Swapp); rub-ons (American Crafts, Scrapworks); paint (Delta, Plaid)

THIS little girlie went to tHE market...

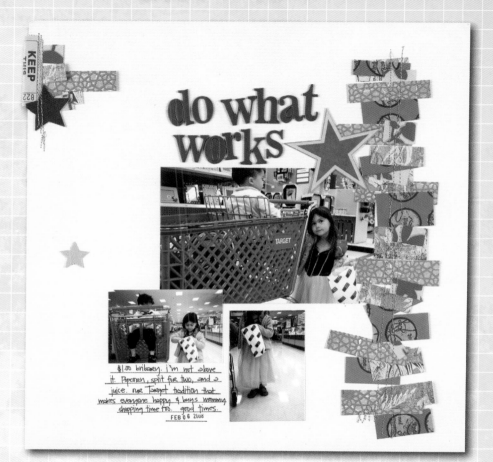

# do what works

$1.00 bribery. i'm not above it. Popcorn, split for two, and a juice. our Target tradition that makes everyone happy & buys mommy shopping time too. good times.

FEB 06 2006

Michelle Ramirez

**Supplies:** Patterned paper (7gypsies, BasicGrey, Fontwerks, KI Memories, Rouge de Garance); chipboard letters (Heidi Swapp); chipboard stars (Imagination Project); Misc: ink, pen, thread

Photo by Becky Novacek

 Becca Sutton

**Supplies:** Patterned paper (7gypsies, BasicGrey, Bazzill, Cosmo Cricket, K&Co., My Mind's Eye, Scenic Route); letter stickers (Making Memories); rub-on frame (Imaginisce); button (Autumn Leaves)

these girls are

the Recipe for laughter

beccа, gigi, becky & me
omaha, nebraska
11·2007

*Photo by Becky Novacek*

**Kerry Lynn Yeary**

**Supplies:** Cardstock (Bazzill); chipboard letters, patterned paper, rub-on letters (October Afternoon); rub-on design (Hambly); felt (Fancy Pants); buttons (Autumn Leaves); brads, tag (Making Memories); flowers (American Crafts, Making Memories); floss (Karen Foster)

17

# Change + Blue-Green + Celery Green

Both green shades can bring to mind different ideas: the ocean, a favorite T-shirt, dollar bills. Combine those thoughts with the word *change* and now what comes to mind? How about the changing tide, changing clothes or change in your pocket? When you receive a prompt, consider how the colors alter your original thoughts when paired. The changes might surprise you!

## Claudine Hellmuth

Reading the prompt, I thought of changing clothes, then good life changes and bad changes, which then led me to thoughts of a bad haircut I got when I was little. I got my hair cut at the cheap chain-store hairdresser's, and I hated it. I cried and cried. While I was working on this piece I wanted to focus in closely on the photo of me getting a haircut and the instant I knew it was a bad idea. And I loved working with the celery and blue-green color combination from the prompt.

**Supplies:** Canvas (Art Alternatives); acrylic paint, glue, pen (Claudine Hellmuth Studio by Ranger); Misc: fabric, tissue paper

### Donna Downey

I cannot get enough of these two colors and was most excited about the theme. I searched through my photos and found several unused wallet-size pictures from projects I had already completed. The photos chronologically represented the changes in my daughter McKenna, so they were perfect for the prompt.

**Supplies:** Cardstock (Bazzill, Die Cuts With A View); letter stickers (Me & My Big Ideas); punches (EK Success); buttons (Autumn Leaves, BasicGrey); rub-on (Hambly)

at Age 5
she was
diff-
icult{

★ Place Alison's party ★

→ → → → →

Date Alison's party
MAY 2004

Lauryn was stubborn
& pushing her
boundaries with her
parents & us ... all the
time. we knew it was a
phase, so were patient
and waited her out.

Christina Lazar-Schuler

The first thing that popped into my mind were the changes a child goes through both physically and emotionally. I used transparencies, which allowed me to see through the pages to the screen-printed patterns, which changed and altered the previous, current and preceding pages in interesting and complex ways.

**Supplies:** Album (American Crafts); transparencies (Hambly, Lazar StudioWerx); patterned paper (BasicGrey); labels (7gypsies, Maya Road); rub-ons (Jenni Bowlin); sticker accents (Chatterbox); Misc: Cream Soda and Daiquiri fonts

### Genevieve Simmonds

*Change* is a pretty big word for me. I'm trying to learn to embrace it and know that it can be a very good thing. I wanted a little bit of the journaling about change hidden on this layout but still readable if someone wanted to get into all that, so I obscured it with some ultra-thick vellum and fabric.

**Supplies:** Cardstock (Bazzill); fabric (Amy Butler); rub-ons (7gypsies, Making Memories); Misc: gesso, masking tape, staples

Kal Barteski

It was fall when I read this prompt, and while I was thinking about the word *change,* I realized that even though the leaves change and the seasons change, the basic structure of a tree stays the same. It's just like those people in my life that no matter what's happening or how life is moving in different directions the relationship never changes too much.

**Supplies:** Chipboard; colored pencils (Prismacolor); acrylic paint (Chroma); ink, stamps (Martha Stewart); pen (Sanford)

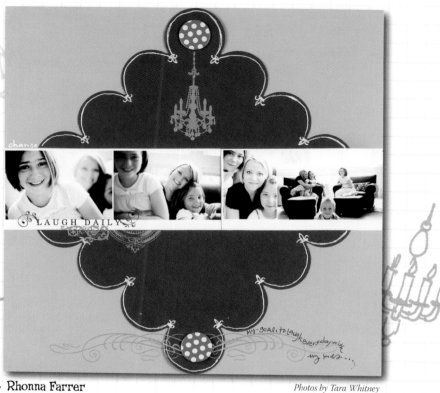

### Rhonna Farrer

*Photos by Tara Whitney*

Change is always hard for me, so to get my creative process going, I focused on the colors. They aren't ones I use normally, so I had to step out of my comfort zone. Change is good! Then my creative process took me to the scalloped brown cardstock. It comes in a 12˝ × 12˝ (30cm × 30cm) square, which I love, but the prompt is *change*, right? So I cut it smaller to frame my photo strip.

**Supplies:** Brads, cardstock (Bazzill); rub-ons (Hambly); digital swirls by Rhonna Farrer (Two Peas in a Bucket); Misc: pen

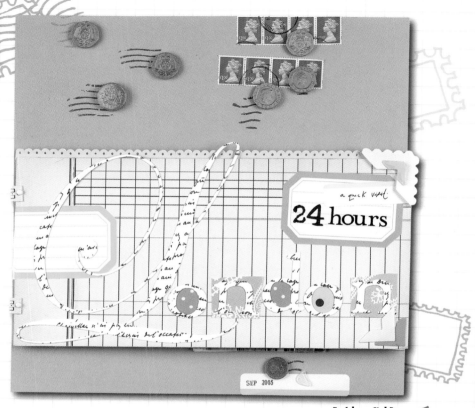

a quick visit

## 24 hours

SEP 2005

**Ashley Calder**

My immediate inclination was to base a page on evolution. But I came across a tin of coins I saved from our trip to London two years ago and recalled all of the photos I had not yet scrapped. I decided to use change as inspiration to use my pocket change on a layout of that brief trip.

**Supplies:** Cardstock, envelopes (Bazzill); patterned paper (Anna Griffin, DMD); labels, rub-ons, stamps (Autumn Leaves); hinges (Making Memories); ribbon (May Arts)

# Gallery

never change how you FEEL ABOUT YOUR brother & he will be your BEST FRIEND forever

Becky Olsen

**Supplies:** Overlays (Hambly); letter stickers (American Crafts); decorative tape (Scrap In Style); rhinestones (Heidi Swapp); rub-ons (American Crafts, Scrapworks); paint (Delta, Plaid)

have
changed
...

no more
**FRAGILE**

my vision of life has
totally changed since my sister passed
away. I realized that life is short and
that I need to do what I really want
to. cease the day. Love. Live. Create.
travel. Laugh. Smile.
make people happy.

Celine Navarro

**Supplies:** Patterned paper, overlay (Hambly); acrylic paint (Making Memories, Ranger); crackle paint (Ranger); letter stickers (American Crafts); rub-ons (American Crafts, BasicGrey, Hambly); stamps (Hero Arts, Stampers Anonymous); flower (Prima); buttons (Autumn Leaves); ribbon (American Crafts)

*Photo by Shannon Wright*

### Kayla Aimee Terrell

**Supplies:** Patterned paper (Making Memories, Scrap In Style); transparency (Hambly); letter stickers (American Crafts, Heidi Swapp, Making Memories); tickets (Jenni Bowlin); sticker accents (Reminisce); labels (Scenic Route); flowers, paint, photo corners (Making Memories); brads (American Crafts); Misc: vintage graph paper, playing card, sheet music

SOMETIMES I FEEL LIKE A...

BROKEN doll baby

Michelle Bernard-Harmazinski

**Supplies:** Cardboard; acrylic paint (Ranger); chipboard letters (Heidi Swapp, Zsiage); letter stickers (Dèjá Views); stamp (Leavenworth Jackson); acrylic tiles (Junkitz); flowers (Michaels); Misc: gesso, ink, pen, ribbon

# Twist + Orange + Coral Pink

A bird's nest, tulle, shoelaces and a puppy dog are all very different and unlikely ideas the designers realized after receiving the prompt *twist*. Grab a pen and make a list: What memories, ideas and thoughts do the word *twist* conjure up for you? Do orange and coral pink draw out special memories, deep emotions or happy times? Be inspired!

## Claudine Hellmuth

The prompt led me down a long "twisty" road to this idea. My first thought: candy with twisted wrappers. Then I made a list of things that twist, like gymnastics and drink straws. I also thought of twisting hair to make a braid, which led me to thoughts of my friend Heather. I remembered that her mom taught me how to tie my shoes; and that memory became the start of his piece. I felt the orange and coral pink cried out for a little turquoise to accompany them for contrast. This project was a lot of fun!

**Supplies:** Canvas (Art Alternative); paper (Provo Craft); acrylic paint, glue, pen (Claudine Hellmuth Studio by Ranger)

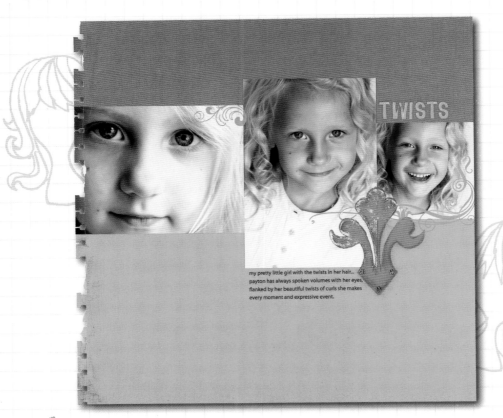

TWISTS

my pretty little girl with the twists in her hair...
payton has always spoken volumes with her eyes,
flanked by her beautiful twists of curls she makes
every moment and expressive event.

### Donna Downey

Given the theme of twist, all I could keep thinking about were the ring curls my daughter gets in her hair with the humidity. I found several photos of her wavy hair and with the color palette already in hand, this page was a cinch!

**Supplies:** Cardstock (Bazzill); letter stickers (Junkitz); rub-ons (Hambly); stamp (Imaginisce); spiral punch (Stampin' Up); rhinestones (Heidi Swapp); paint (Making Memories)

Kal Barteski

The word *twist* made me think of a story with an unexpected ending. I thought blue was missing from the mix of orange and pink, which immediately brought bluebirds to mind. All that made the blackbird pie nursery rhyme pop into my head, and all of a sudden the bluebirds were flying out of a pie—all of which seemed like a perfect twist for the prompt.

**Supplies:** Chipboard; colored pencils (Prismacolor); acrylic paint (Chroma); ink, stamps (Martha Stewart); pen (Sanford)

## Rhonna Farrer

*Photo by Tara Whitney*

Tara Whitney is one of my all-time favorite photographers, so my whole creative process for this project began with the photo. My arms were wrapped around my daughter and it made me think of *twist.* So I ran with it. I twisted tulle. I twisted my pen around in my hand to create swirls. I twisted the brads into the flowers. I twisted my scissors as I cut out the digital scrapbook stickers. I twisted the colors together!

**Supplies:** Cardstock (Bazzill); rub-ons (Autumn Leaves); rhinestones (Queen & Co.); flowers (American Crafts, Heidi Swapp); brads (Autumn Leaves); digital swirls by Rhonna Farrer (Two Peas in a Bucket); Misc: calligraphy pen, tulle

**Genevieve Simmonds**

I was working on this prompt and having a hard time coming up with a concept. I looked down at my desk and saw the first photos of our new puppy and how she was all over the place. Right away I thought "twisting to and fro," and this little poem came to me. The rest was a snap. Sometimes photos can be such awesome inspiration.

**Supplies:** Cardstock (Bazzill); letter stickers (EK Success, Heidi Swapp); heart sticker (Heidi Grace); buttons (My Mind's Eye); Misc: Violation font, sequins

Within the image: handwritten text "winter 2007/08", "going down the highway, or spotted across a field, i see bird's nests. and i love them.", "the nest found (Keswick) and the nest not laid in (Dundee)", and "and in a tree there was a nest"

## Ashley Calder

My train of thought took me through the words *turn, entwine, knit* and finally *nest*. I decided to focus my page on my new favorite collection: these beautiful little natural works of twisted twigs, grass and mud—birds' nests! I even included a piece of broken nest I found in the park.

**Supplies:** Patterned paper (7gypsies, Hambly); frame, rub-ons (Making Memories); tags (Jenni Bowlin); rhinestone (Westrim); chipboard accents (Maya Road); photo corners (American Crafts, Heidi Swapp); Misc: vintage book page, postage stamp

### Christina Lazar-Schuler

I knew how I would work with this color palette, but the theme was another matter. So instead of being literal in using the *twist* prompt as a jumping-off point for the subject, I twisted the idea of a scrapbook page and created a triptych of framed layouts. In the end, the twist for me was to take the traditional and shake it up!

**Supplies:** Frames (Ikea); patterned paper (Lazar StudioWERX); rub-ons, transparency (Hambly); letter stickers (American Crafts); brads (Making Memories); labels (7gypsies); flowers, ticket stubs (Jenni Bowlin); chipboard shapes (Maya Road)

# Gallery

they were not the plan

I like to plan things out. Next weekend or 5 years from now, I like to know what's going to happen. My plan was not twins we weren't even sure we wanted more than one kid. But life (ie, GOD) threw us a twist— twins. And I couldn't be more thankful. Sometimes (often) our plans are nothing compared to what He has for us. 8/07

**Melanie McFarlin**

**Supplies:** Cardstock; patterned paper (Scenic Route); letter stickers (American Crafts); felt trim (Fancy Pants)

i
control
my
destiny

not a simple twist of fate

i have a dream and that dream
is all mine - i control it. i can
make it a reality
it has already happened
i just need to take the
steps, follow the dream!

**Courtney DeLaura**

**Supplies:** Patterned paper,
ribbon (Martha Stewart);
brad (American Crafts)

Dear Jana...

## vital NecessiTy

Whatever our souls
are made of,
yours and mine
are the same.

South Africa, Sept 2007
Picture by Martin.

i love this picture of you. You are so carefree and happy here... my hearts desire is for you to always be happy... thats why its vital for you to line up your thoughts with Gods thoughts. Don't ever give up because little by little you are changing. The more you change your mind for the better, the more you change your life for the better. When you begin to see things than for you in your thinking you will begin to walk in it. Rom 12:2 says - don't be conformed to this world, fashioned after and adapted to its external superficial customs, but be renewed in your mind by its new ideals and its new attitude, so that you may prove for yourself what is the good and acceptable and perfect will of God. So dear Jana ... its of a vital necessity that you would keep on renewing your mind until you are old... i love you...

Love Wilna

29 January 2008.

## Wilna Furstenberg

**Supplies:** Cardstock (Bazzill); patterned paper, tags, transparency (My Mind's Eye); chipboard letters, paint, paper clip (Making Memories)

**ALL GIRL**

**girly girl**

*princess*

girls rule pink stuff play laugh

PEARL HARBOR
THE DIRECTOR'S CUT

13 going on 30

failure to launch

FERRIS BUELLER'S DAY OFF
BUELLER ... BUELLER ... EDITION

MEAN GIRLS

SECONDHAND LIONS

THE COUNT OF Monte Cristo

THE FAMILY STONE

A WALK TO REMEMBER

MY BIG FAT GREEK WEDDING

HOME ALONE

The Sweetest Thing

NOTEBOOK

10 things I hate about you

TALLADEGA NIGHTS
THE BALLAD OF RICKY BOBBY

SWEET HOME ALABAMA

AUSTIN POWERS International Man of Mystery

THREE AMIGOS

DUMB and DUMBER

WEDDING CRASHERS UNCORKED

MR. DEEDS

A KNIGHT'S TALE

HITCH

HOW TO LOSE A GUY IN 10 DAYS

SLEEPLESS IN SEATTLE

my **FAVS**

{movies-that is}

sappy love stories
Romantic
comedies

funny movies!

nothing scary
or violent

if it is girly I
love it!
the girlier the
better actually!

-2008

## Gretchen McElveen

**Supplies:** Cardstock (Bazzill); patterned paper (Creative Imaginations, My Mind's Eye, Urban Lily); chipboard letters, letter stickers (American Crafts); buttons (Autumn Leaves); paint (Heidi Swapp); tag (Jenni Bowlin)

# Play + Cyan + Purple

Believe it or not, artwork about a spider, a violin and an iPod all resulted from the word *play*! At least two of us didn't like the color purple when we started this prompt, but when pushed to create with a color we didn't like the result was exciting! Don't be afraid to play with new colors—accept the challenge and you might surprise yourself.

## Claudine Hellmuth

I don't really like purple, so at first I ignored the color and focused on *play* and the things it brought to mind, like playing an instrument. I remembered my grade school violin lessons—I am practically tone deaf so those were a nightmare. To make matters worse, at my recital, my bow became knotted in my violin and had to just stand there! After painting a purple background for the piece and hating it, I was happy to discover some papers with a blue and purple pattern that worked perfectly for my dress and eased my mind about the color palette.

**Supplies:** Canvas (Art Alternatives); paper (Provo Craft, unknown); acrylic paint, glue, pen (Claudine Hellmuth Studio by Ranger)

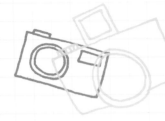

### Genevieve Simmonds

I had to make use of these crazy, silly photos of my son Jaxon playing. I was so glad to have my camera handy on this particular day. The light was beautiful in his room, and we were having so much fun. I wanted the page to be fun and happy too, so I used bright embellishments that would stand out along with the photos on the neutral cardstock.

**Supplies:** Cardstock (Bazzill); sticker accents (Provo Craft); rub-on letters (office supply store); Misc: fiber

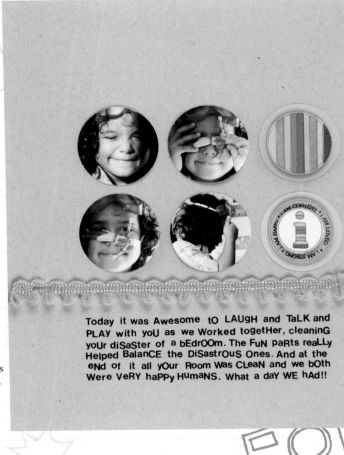

Today it was Awesome to LAUgH and TaLK and PLAY with yoU as we Worked togetHer, cleaninG yOur diSaSter of a bEdrOOm. The FuN paRts reaLLy Helped BalanCE the DiSastrOuS Ones. And at the eNd of it all yOur Room Was CLeaN and we bOth Were VeRY haPPy HumaNS. What a daY WE hAd!!

**Ashley Calder**

What springs to mind when I hear the word *play*? My girls playing. For something that happens daily, all day, this is something I have few layouts of. So I made a layout of my youngest daughter playing with her marble run. I punched circles of patterned paper and added letters to spell *roll* repeatedly, and my journaling bounced and rolled down the page.

**Supplies:** Cardstock (Bazzill); patterned paper (Anna Griffin, KI Memories, Rhonna Designs, Scenic Route); letter stickers (K&Co.); plastic stars (American Crafts); watercolors (Winsor & Newton); brads (Making Memories); Misc: iridescent medium, matte gel

still love playing with my sisters...

even as adults

PLAY
laugh

photo op

we still get together & laugh till we cry...i love them!

### Rhonna Farrer

Whenever I get together with my sisters, we laugh and laugh. These women make me feel young! I loved creating a scrapbook page with fun, playful pictures of myself and my sisters. I used some playful layering techniques along with playful swirls to enhance the joyful feeling.

**Supplies:** Digital brush, die-cuts, grid transparency, labels, photo frame, patterned paper, tape by Rhonna Farrer (Two Peas in a Bucket)

peek a boo!

play!

## Donna Downey

When I first saw the prompt, I was worried because I am not a big fan of purple. As I started going through my paints, I decided to find a shade of purple that made me happy. I painted the pages of this mini album and from there chose photos that represented my kids at play. I kept the embellishments simple, and I am really happy with the results!

**Supplies:** Mini album (7gypsies); paint (Making Memories, Plaid); rub-ons (BasicGrey, Hambly) journaling tags (Heidi Swapp)

## Christina Lazar-Schuler

I spend lots of time playing my iPod and creating playlists, so *play* inspired an iPod playlist mini album. The cyan and purple color palette is not one I work with often. Fortunately, it was one of the palettes of some new digital papers I designed. Talk about serendipity! I used mini chipboard arrows to further "play" up the iPod play idea because the foundation of an iPod's navigation is arrows.

**Supplies:** Chipboard sheets (Bazzill); patterned paper (BasicGrey); transparencies (Hambly); digital paper (Lazar StudioWerx); letter stickers (American Crafts, Chatterbox); chipboard arrows (Maya Road); labels (7gypsies, Jenni Bowlin)

ME.
PLAY WITH
ME.

oh HOW
HOW

· WAS IT SUCH A
TERRIBLE THING THAT
SHE ONLY wanted to play

WAS iT
SO TERRIBLE

OR WERE HER TEARS invisible ?

PLAY

play

K.BARTESKI 2007.

OH LET HER play.

Kal Barteski

The colors reminded me of a rainy day, and the rainy day made me think of boys playing outside, which caused my brain to jump over to the kid that no one wants to play
with. And that made me think of spiders—a black widow spider to be exact and how it
must be lonely to be a widow and to be a spider.

**Supplies:** Chipboard; colored pencils (Prismacolor); acrylic paint (Chroma); ink, stamps (Martha Stewart);
pen (Sanford)

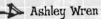

**Ashley Wren**

**Supplies:** Cardstock; die-cut paper, patterned paper (KI Memories); letter sticker (7gypsies); star trim (Jenni Bowlin)

She really knows how to 2008

PLAY

a tune, as I watched her in Old Town San Diego near the Whaley House

Adrienne Looman

**Supplies:** Cardstock (Bazzill); journaling rub-on, overlay (Hambly); flowers (Prima); brads (American Crafts); embellishments (KI Memories); Misc: pen

HAD SO MUCH fun, running in the sand...finding shells... jumping in the waves...riding me boogie board... listening to the waves building sand castles played all day

LOVED it from the very start...

OH Yeah... She's a Big Fan now...

Miss Kelly Rose meets the ocean for me 1st time...

hello awesome

OBX

July 2006

## Gigi Kennedy

**Supplies:** Cardstock (Bazzill); letter stickers (American Crafts); buttons, stamp (Autumn Leaves); chipboard flowers, ribbons (Making Memories); Misc: ink, pen

Sarah Bowen

**Supplies:** Chipboard; patterned paper (BasicGrey); chipboard letters (American Crafts); brads (Making Memories); label (7gypsies); star sequins (Wal-Mart)

53

# Dress + Yellow + Green

The word *dress* can trigger so many memories: a big dance, childhood make-believe or a night out on the town. Pair the word *dress* with the colors yellow and green, and it can change the outcome of the word prompt. Are you now imagining spring dresses or a summer wedding? After considering a word or color on its own, think of them together to see if they prompt entirely different ideas or memories.

## Claudine Hellmuth

For the *dress* prompt, I thought first of an Easter dress and dressing up for special occasions, but then my mind led me to thoughts of playing dress up. When I was little, I had an English bulldog named George, who was one of my best playmates. He endured many hours of dress up, so I created a piece around that theme in tribute to George and his patience!

**Supplies:** Canvas (Art Alternatives); paper (Die Cuts With A View, Scrap In Style); watercolor pencils (Loew Cornell); acrylic paint, glue, pen (Claudine Hellmuth Studio by Ranger)

*Photo by Tara Whitney*

### Rhonna Farrer

For this digital layout, I wanted the focus on my daughter's cute little piggies, which happened to be peaking out of a light green dress. I kept the page background neutral, but added a few green elements and some feminine details. I created a frame around the photo with some digital brushes. I also added digital stickers, tape, labels, swirls and text.

**Supplies:** Digital brushes, frames, labels, paper, stickers, tape by Rhonna Farrer (Two Peas in a Bucket); Misc: AL Modern Type and Blackmoor fonts

Photos by Match Studio Photography

*Handwritten journaling on page:*

i felt so beautiful in my wedding dress! and tony looked at me with such pride and love

Everyone know... as much as the BIG day is about us, it's also about the dress. Mine was lovely, soft and completely unique... it was custom made...

**Christina Lazar-Schuler**

The first thing I thought of when I read *dress* was my wedding dress. I'm not a "girly girl" so it is the most significant dress in my life. I cross-processed my photos with a green tinge to give them a unique, fresh look and also to tie in the color scheme, one that evokes spring, new beginnings and a new life—like marriage.

**Supplies:** Acrylic album (Lazar StudioWerx); letter stickers (American Crafts); sticker accents (Chatterbox, Heidi Swapp); labels (7gypsies, Maya Road); rub-ons (BasicGrey, Hambly, Jenni Bowlin); Misc: jump rings, pens

## Donna Downey

This was the final project I completed for this book, and I knew exactly what I wanted to do. I just had to find the right picture to do it with! My daughter likes to dress up, usually as a fairy princess, so she has several pairs of wings we have acquired over the years. I had this vision of capturing a moment with her in wings, which led to this "time in a bottle" dressed in green.

**Supplies:** Jar (Ball); wing stamps (Endless Creations); acrylic paint, ink (Ranger); ribbon (Making Memories); rub-ons (7gypsies, BasicGrey, Hambly, Heidi Swapp); Misc: batting, fabric, marbles, tulle

Kal Barteski

When I saw the word *dress*, a clothesline with white cotton dresses popped into my mind. But I'm not a dress person, so the clothesline full of dresses turned into a clothesline full of socks and underwear. And then I pictured really ugly orange wool socks. It seemed that the only connection these socks had to a dress is that they shouldn't be worn together—unless it was by someone eccentric.

**Supplies:** Chipboard; colored pencils (Prismacolor); acrylic paint (Chroma); ink, stamps (Martha Stewart); pen (Sanford)

### Genevieve Simmonds

I'm totally in love with the color palette for this prompt! A little while ago I went out with friends for a birthday, and we had our makeup professionally done first. The makeup was green and sparkly and so much fun, inspiring me to dress up and feel great. I don't get out often, so that night of sushi and sake, drinks at Lolita's and hitting reggae night at the club was all the sweeter!

**Supplies:** Cardstock (Bazzill); patterned paper (American Crafts, Scenic Route); labels (7gypsies, Fontwerks); letter stickers cut from decorative tape (7gypsies)

dress up. rock out

Jen w/ makeup by gus. Jerome's bday 2007.

makeup by gus
dinner @ tappa
drinks @ liz's
reggae night
dancing dancing

ON THE 31st

SHE WORE her CAT COSTUME and she wore it WELL

### Ashley Calder

I thought about the idea of dressing yourself in an image, a guise or a costume. These photos of my daughter Addie Blue dressed up as a cat suited the idea so well. Not only did she dress herself in that cat costume, but she really *dressed* herself. She wore that cat costume, and she became that cat!

**Supplies:** Cardstock (Bazzill); letter stickers (Making Memories); buttons, stamp, transparency (Autumn Leaves); tags (Li'l Davis, Making Memories); ribbon (Making Memories, Wrights); vellum (DMD); photo corners (Anna Griffin, Canson, Heidi Swapp); brads (Autumn Leaves, Making Memories); watercolors (Winsor & Newton); Misc: floss

# Gallery

**Lisa Garay**

**Supplies:** Patterned paper (American Crafts, BasicGrey, Creative Imaginations, Daisy D's, Hambly, KI Memories, Making Memories, My Mind's Eye, Prima); buttons (Autumn Leaves); ribbon (We R Memory Keepers); flowers (Prima); stickers (7gypsies, American Crafts); Misc: brads

the
forgotten

**dress**

Great Gramma Chapman sent me this dress
from England when I was born... 34 years ago.
I always wanted to save it and have my
baby girls wear it. Unfortunately, it
was forgotten about, being it was
dressed on a doll in storage for years. The
dress is now safely tucked away waiting for
my Grand· daughter, way to plan! Praise
God for little treasures to think upon.

### Andrea Wiebe

**Supplies:** Cardstock
(Bazzill); patterned paper
(Imaginisce); letter stickers
(American Crafts); but-
terfly, flowers (Maya Road);
tag (Staples); Misc: buttons,
floss, ink, lace, notepaper

I never realised How My Clothes Reflected How Comfortable My Mind is! High heels And Confidence, Pjs and Hiding... How hard it is to put on a Cocktail dress for a date When really you Want to hide. Wearing Jeans + flip flops in the SuperMarket and Meeting An old friend Who is Glam And Happy, now that is really a time to examine Your life! Maybe first I need to learn Comfort with Me!

**who am i**

**today**

DRESS

### Jo-Anne te Raa

**Supplies:** Acrylic paint (Ranger); letter stickers (American Crafts); button (K&Co.); rub-ons (Hambly); paper doll and clothes (vintage Judy Garland toy); Misc: wooden chest, vintage dress pattern book

love finds

a new chance
a new start

happiness
bliss

inside your ♥

a new address

love again, 2008

Bernadette Henderson

**Supplies:** Digital buttons, frames, heart, lace, paper, tags, staples (Digital Design Essentials); cardboard edge by Linda Billdal (ScrapArtist); chipboard letters, stitching by Katie Pertiet (Designer Digitals)

# Shine + Blue + Orange

Does the word *shine* along with the colors blue and orange make you think of light modes in Photoshop? It did for one of our designers! Another artist thought of the highlight in a person's eye while another's thoughts went to Christmas Day. Who would have thought that the word *shine* would elicit so many individual ideas and interesting memories? I'm sure you'll agree the designers offer plenty of intriguing illustrations for interpreting this prompt.

## Claudine Hellmuth

When I read the prompt, I couldn't think of anything right away. After letting the word sit in my mind, I thought of the phrase "she took a shine to him." Suddenly I knew what I would do—a piece about my husband and me smitten with each other. Finding the just-right photos required a search though various albums. I wanted to use childhood photos, and once I found the perfect ones, I created the piece to show us holding hands.

**Supplies:** Canvas (Art Alternatives); paper (Die Cuts With A View); watercolor pencils (Loew Cornell); acrylic paint, glue, pen (Claudine Hellmuth Studio by Ranger)

## Ashley Calder

While looking through photos with *shine* in mind, I was struck by these Christmas pictures. Not only does the tree shine, but the girls do, too. To incorporate the colors, I layered blue liquid ink over a yellow and orange acrylic background. For shine, I applied iridescent medium with a brayer over the ink and dusted gold and silver leaf on top of the page.

**Supplies:** Chipboard; chipboard letters (Heidi Swapp); letter stickers (Making Memories); stamps (Autumn Leaves, Ma Vinci); gold and silver leafing, ink (Stewart Superior); paper frill (Doodlebug); rhinestones (Westrim); photo corners (American Crafts); iridescent medium for watercolors (Winsor & Newton); Misc: acrylic paint, ink

**Donna Downey**

I knew I wanted to create a piece about my daughter when I read the prompt. I have been working on stretched canvas a lot lately, so I began with a blank canvas and painted one half blue and the other half orange. At this point, I didn't really know where the project was headed; I was just playing around. I glued the photo to the canvas and continued to add the rest of the elements playing off the color theme.

**Supplies:** Canvas (Dick Blick); acrylic paint (Making Memories); chipboard accents (Maya Road); stamps (Stampers Anonymous); rub-ons (Hambly); Misc: ink

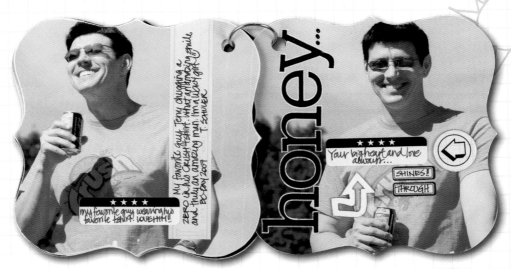

My favorite guy. Terry chugging a zero while CRUSHin' his shirt. What an amazing smile and truly an amazing man. I'm a lucky girl! Lynette
BC-Day 2007     T. Schuler

honey...

★★★★
my favorite guy wearing his favorite tshirt! LOVE HIM!!

★★★★
Your big heart and love always...

SHINES!

THROUGH

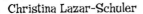

## Christina Lazar-Schuler

This color combination was a fun one, and it perfectly suited the photos I wanted to use. Who could have predicted that my husband would wear the perfect orange T-shirt on a sunny, clear, blue-skied summer day? Who could have predicted that these photos, taken at the spur of the moment, would so perfectly match this prompt? Certainly not me! I couldn't have planned it better if I tried.

**Supplies:** Patterned paper (Lazar StudioWerx); letter stickers, sticker accents (American Crafts); chipboard arrows (Maya Road); labels (7gypsies, Chatterbox, Jenni Bowlin); Misc: album

shine
Baby... you
when you smile!

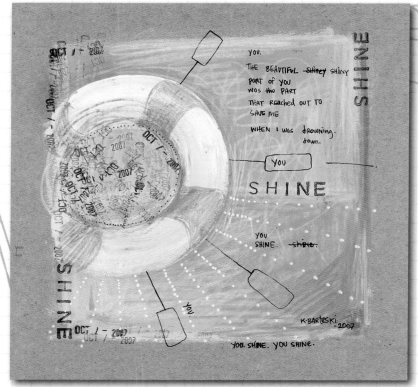

Kal Barteski

When I saw the word *shine*, I immediately thought of the highlight of a person's eye—especially when they're laughing or crying. A few key moments and people in my life came to mind, and the more I thought about them the more I saw their contribution as something that "pulled me up" or saved me. So, from *shine* I took a zigzag pattern to the image of an eye, to a circle, to a life preserver. Seemed perfectly logical at the time.

**Supplies:** Chipboard; colored pencils (Prismacolor); acrylic paint (Chroma); ink, stamps (Martha Stewart); pen (Sanford)

### Genevieve Simmonds

This layout was already in the works when I chose to use it for the prompt. My husband and I have few photos together, so even though this is not the best photo of us, I wanted to use it because it captured a moment and a memory for me. (He is so cute!) The journaling was the part I got stuck on, but when I thought of the word *shine*, it was the perfect inspiration to complete the page.

**Supplies:** Patterned paper (BasicGrey); letter stickers (SEI); labels (7gypsies, Fontwerks); Misc: masking tape, mesh, staples, wrapping paper

Rhonna Farrer

One of the great things about Photoshop is the set of various light modes you can use to make things shine. On this layout, I applied the overlay light mode over the face in the top corner to give it a blown-out look. Over the center face I used the multiply light mode to blend it. The face in the frame has text, swirls and part of the Eiffel Tower photograph blended with various light modes to give it an ethereal quality.

**Supplies:** Digital kit by Rhonna Farrer (Two Peas in a Bucket); adhesive paper (Avery)

# Gallery

GATHER SIBLINGS FOR MEETING
DICIDE ON TEA PARTY FOR MOTHERS DAY
RETRIEVE GOOD SILVER TEA SET
OH DARN-ITS DIRTY
WISE OLDEST SISTER KNOWS THAT SOS PADS CAN MAKE ANYTHING SHINE
MOM IS VERY SUPRISED
ESPECIALLY AT HOW shiney
HER SILVER TEA SET IS
THE LOOK ON HER FACE WHEN SHE SEES
THE SOS PADS OUT
SAYS IT ALL

A MOTHER'S DAY she'll nEver forGET!

S.O.S Magic Scouring Pads
NEW OVAL

**Diane Dolan**

**Supplies:** Canvas; Grungeboard letters and accents (Tim Holtz); acrylic dots (Cloud 9); labels (Dymo); Misc: vintage ephemera

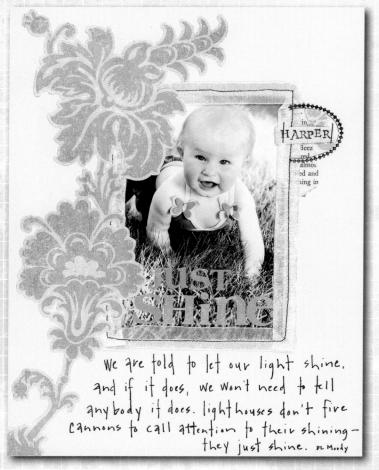

HARPER

in
Beez
red
almos
ed and
ning in

JUST
SHINE

We are told to let our light shine.
and if it does, we won't need to tell
anybody if does. lighthouses don't fire
cannons to call attention to their shining—
they just shine. DL Moody

**Becky Novacek**

**Supplies:** Letter stickers, patterned paper (BasicGrey); rub-ons (7gypsies); stamps (Hero Arts)

I love the way you shine.

Ava

### Jody Ferlaak

**Supplies:** Patterned paper (BasicGrey, K&Co., Scrap In Style); chipboard letters and accents (Making Memories); decorative punches (EK Success, McGill); felt (Fancy Pants); photo corners (Heidi Swapp); sticker (Fontwerks)

allie we are so happy that you found something that you love so much. You normally are so shy & reserved, but when you put on your ballet shoes & tutu there is an unmistakable sparkle & shine about you.

On the 1st day of dance several parents & even your teacher asked where you had previously taken dance. The only answer I could come up with was .... " the school of Twelve Dancing Princesses."

Kelli Darr

**Supplies:** Cardstock (Bazzill); glitter letters (Target); rhinestones, ribbon (Heidi Swapp)

# About the Design Team

### Kal Barteski

Kal's trademark—her fearless and generous approach to art, illustration and print design—has won her national and international design awards. Working fluidly in a variety of media including pencil crayon, acrylic, chalk, watercolors, oil, pencil, ink, scrapbooking, photography, words and digital pieces, she is an energetic, enthusiastic and colorful art-maker with a unique and contagious passion.

Today she's juggling time between design and painting as she strives for a life well-lived with her husband, Dan, daughter, Pilot, boxer dog, Crash, and whatever colorful adventures come their way.

*www.lovelife.typepad.com*

### Ashley Calder

Ashley is a mixed-media scrapbooker. She lives in Dundas, Ontario, Canada with daughters Summer Lily and Addison Blue, husband Paul, and cats Delilah and Murial. Her debut book, *Scraptastic!*, was released in fall 2007 by Memory Makers Books.

*www.ashleycalder.blogspot.com*

### Donna Downey

As the author of the innovative book series, Yes, It's a Scrapbook! and columnist for *Simple Scrapbooks* magazine, Donna is a craft and paper product junkie. She and enjoys traveling across the globe teaching at scrapbook stores and events, writing books, gathering inspiration, designing and endorsing products, as well as doing guest expert appearances on QVC. Originally from the Jersey shore, Donna now lives in North Carolina with her husband, Bill ,and their three children, McKenna, Payton and Cole.

*www.donnadowney.com*
*www.donnadowney.typepad.com*

## Rhonna Farrer

Rhonna was inducted into the Creating Keepsakes' Hall of Fame in 2004 as a digital scrapbooker and since then has found her new love: combining digital with traditional scrapbooking. She was a part of the Scrapbooks, Etc. 2007 creative team, and now serves on the Creative Advisory Board of Shutterfly.com.

She uses her digital art to design product lines with Autumn Leaves. She also loves working with the Two Peas in a Bucket Web site as a design team member and designing digital kits for the site. Rhonna loves teaching and inspiring both traditional and digital scrapbookers all over the world.

*www.rhonnadesigns.com*

## Christina Lazar-Schuler

Christina is the owner/creative director of Lazar StudioWERX, a Canadian manufacturer of fine art rubber stamps, hand-painted printed papers and the Claudine Hellmuth Poppets® product line. In addition to her paper arts business and artwork, Christina is an accomplished mixed media artist designer and workshop instructor. Christina teaches classes in mixed media with subject matter covering image/Polaroid transfer, acrylic painting, collage, collage quilting and altered books. She is excited about this opportunity to share her techniques with scrapbookers, hoping to push them out into a place of experimentation and discovery.

*www.lazarstudiowerx.com*

## Claudine Hellmuth

See author bio on page 2.

## Genevieve Simmonds

Gen is a mixed-media, outside-the-box scrapbooker who just plain loves making a mess and making art. She is a member of The Dares and co-author of *We Dare You*, published by Memory Makers Books, and has had the pleasure of painting and designing paper with Lazar StudioWERX. She lives with her beloved husband and son in Vancouver, British Columbia, Canada.

*www.genevievesimmonds.typepad.com*

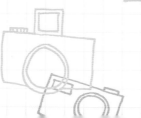

# source guide

The following companies manufacture products featured in this book. Please check your local retailers or go to a company's Web site for the latest product information. In addition, we have made every attempt to properly credit the items mentioned in this book. We apologize to any company that we have listed incorrectly, and we would appreciate hearing from you.

**7gypsies**
www.sevengypsies.com

**American Crafts**
www.americancrafts.com

**Amy Butler Design**
www.amybutlerdesign.com

**Anna Griffin, Inc.**
www.annagriffin.com

**Art Alternatives**
www.art-alternatives.com

**Autumn Leaves**
www.autumnleaves.com

**Avery Dennison Corporation**
www.avery.com

**Ball Corporation**
www.ball.com

**BasicGrey**
www.basicgrey.com

**Bazzill Basics Paper**
www.bazzillbasics.com

**Bind-it-All/Zutter Innovative Products**
www.binditall.com

**Canson, Inc.**
www.canson-us.com

**Caran d'Ache**
www.carandache.com

**Chatterbox, Inc.**
www.chatterboxinc.com

**Chroma Inc.**
www.chromaonline.com

**Claudine Hellmuth Studio** - see Ranger

**Cloud 9 Design**
www.cloud9design.biz

**Cosmo Cricket**
www.cosmocricket.com

**Creative Imaginations**
www.cigift.com

**Daisy D's Paper Company**
www.daisydspaper.com

**Dèjá Views/C-Thru Ruler**
www.dejaviews.com

**Delta Creative, Inc.**
www.deltacreative.com

**Designer Digitals**
www.designerdigitals.com

**Dick Blick Holdings, Inc.**
www.dickblick.com

**Die Cuts With A View**
www.diecutswithaview.com

**Digital Design Essentials**
www.digitaldesignessentials.com

**DMC Corp.**
www.dmc-usa.com

**DMD Paper**
www.creativityinc.com/dmd

**Donna Downey**
www.donnadowney.com

**Doodlebug Design Inc.**
www.doodlebug.ws

**Dymo**
www.dymo.com

**EK Success, Ltd.**
www.eksuccess.com

**Endless Creations Inc.**
www.shopec.com

**Fancy Pants Designs, LLC**
www.fancypantsdesigns.com

**Fontwerks**
www.fontwerks.com

**Hambly Screenprints**
www.hamblyscreenprints.com

**Heidi Grace Designs, Inc.**
www.heidigrace.com

**Heidi Swapp/Advantus Corporation**
www.heidiswapp.com

**Hero Arts Rubber Stamps, Inc.**
www.heroarts.com

**Ikea**
www.ikea.com

**Imagination Project, Inc.**
www.imaginationproject.com

**Imaginisce**
www.imaginisce.com

**Jenni Bowlin**
www.jennibowlin.com

**Junkitz**
www.junkitz.com

**K&Company**
www.kandcompany.com

**Karen Foster Design**
www.karenfosterdesign.com

**KI Memories**
www.kimemories.com

**Lazar Studiowerx, Inc.**
www.lazarstudiowerx.com

**Leavenworth Jackson**
www.ljackson.com

**Li'l Davis Designs**
www.lildavisdesigns.com

**Loew-Cornell**
www.loew-cornell.com

**Ma Vinci's Reliquary**
www.reliquary.cyberstamps.com

**Making Memories**
www.makingmemories.com

**Martha Stewart Crafts**
www.marthastewartcrafts.com

**May Arts**
www.mayarts.com

**Maya Road, LLC**
www.mayaroad.com

**McGill, Inc.**
www.mcgillinc.com

**Me & My Big Ideas**
www.meandmybigideas.com

**Michaels Arts & Crafts**
www.michaels.com

**My Mind's Eye, Inc.**
www.mymindseye.com

**October Afternoon**
www.octoberafternoon.com

**Plaid Enterprises, Inc.**
www.plaidonline.com

**Prima Marketing, Inc.**
www.primamarketinginc.com

**Prismacolor by Sanford**
www.prismacolor.com

**Provo Craft**
www.provocraft.com

**Queen & Co.**
www.queenandcompany.com

**Ranger Industries, Inc.**
www.rangerink.com

**Reminisce Papers**
www.shopreminisce.com

**Rhonna Designs**
www.rhonnadesigns.com

**Rouge de Garance**
www.rougedegarance.com

**Sanford Corporation**
www.sanfordcorp.com

**Scenic Route Paper Co.**
www.scenicroutepaper.com

**Scrap In Style TV**
www.sistvboutique.com

**ScrapArtist**
www.scrapartist.com

**Scrapworks, LLC**
www.scrapworks.com

**SEI, Inc.**
www.shopsei.com

**Speedball Art Products Company**
www.speedballart.com

**Stampers Anonymous**
www.stampersanonymous.com

**Stampin' Up!**
www.stampinup.com

**Staples, Inc.**
www.staples.com

**Stewart Superior Corporation**
www.stewartsuperior.com

**Target**
www.target.com

**Tim Holtz**
www.timholtz.com

**Two Peas in a Bucket**
www.twopeasinabucket.com

**Two's Company**
www.twoscompany.com

**Urban Lily**
www.urbanlily.com

**Wal-Mart Stores, Inc.**
www.walmart.com

**We R Memory Keepers, Inc.**
www.weronthenet.com

**Westrim Crafts**
www.creativityinc.com

**Winsor & Newton**
www.winsornewton.com

**Wrights Ribbon Accents**
www.wrights.com

**Zsiage, LLC**
www.zsiage.com